I know this to be true

Stephen Curry

I know this to be true

_____

on family,
determination
& passion

Interview and photography

Geoff Blackwell

CHRONICLE BOOKS
SAN FRANCISCO

in association with

Blackwell&Ruth.

Dedicated to the legacy
and memory of
Nelson Mandela

'I know what I believe in, and
I know what I stand for. And
I know what I stand against.'

Introduction

When Stephen Curry was a kid, he was introduced to a basketball hoop in Grottoes, Virginia. It wasn't fancy – just a worn utility pole, rough fibreglass backboard and sturdy rim – but his grandpa had built it, and it was where his father, NBA (National Basketball Association) veteran Dell Curry,[i] had honed his craft. Family visits to see his grandma[ii] were dominated by time spent behind the house, taking shots with his younger brother Seth.[iii]

The difficult positioning of the hoop and uneven ground made it the perfect place to test his abilities, but it was thanks to his father that he learned the fundamentals of basketball. When he was young, Dell would take his sons along to his games with the Charlotte Hornets and let them warm up with the team. At home they played for hours on their backyard court, persisting into the night. Only when their mother decided it had been long enough would they retire for the day.

The practice paid off; after playing for Charlotte Christian School as a teenager, Stephen was recruited by Davidson College in North Carolina. It wasn't his first choice – wanting to follow in his father's footsteps, he had hoped to play for the Virginia Tech Hokies,[iv] but was overlooked in part due to his slight frame (at the time he was only about six-foot-one and weighed one hundred and sixty pounds). Things worked out favourably in the end, however. Under Davidson Wildcats coach Bob McKillop, Curry polished his skills and found his calling. In his first year he broke the NCAA (National Collegiate Athletic Association) freshman season record for three-point field goals, and was named SoCon (Southern Conference) Tournament MVP (Most Valuable Player) and SoCon Freshman of the Year. The following year he took Davidson on to win their first NCAA Tournament game in over thirty-five years. 'Going to Davidson, and playing – and winning – at that level of hoops . . . it made me who I am, in a way. It made me understand what it means to build something. Like, truly build something. Something that no one can ever take away from you. Something that's all your own.'[1]

In 2009 he skipped his senior year to enter the NBA draft, marking the end of his time with the Wildcats. By now he was six-foot-three and had filled out somewhat. With experience behind him, he was selected by the Golden State Warriors as the seventh pick, becoming the team's starting point guard. Three NBA championships and more than a decade later, he remains with the Warriors.

Now regarded as one of the greatest basketball shooters of all time – *Sports Illustrated* said that 'the NBA has never seen a shooter like Steph Curry' – Curry doesn't shy from using his platform to address controversial issues.[2] In 2016 after a series of police shootings of African Americans, San Francisco 49ers quarterback Colin Kaepernick gained international attention for sitting in protest during the national anthem. While his actions angered those who felt he was disrespecting the American flag – including the President – they also garnered approval from many. Curry spoke out in support of Kaepernick's bravery, praising him for taking a stand against police brutality towards people of colour and, in doing so, forcing the issue onto the global stage.

A year later, Curry declined an invitation from the president to visit the White House and celebrate the Golden State Warriors'

2017 NBA championship win. Instead, the team took a group of forty elementary school students to the National Museum of African American History in Washington, D.C. 'We wanted to be able to control the narrative around the celebration and conversation of us winning a championship. And not let somebody else who wasn't spreading positivity and love do that for us', he explained.[3]

These principles translate to the home, too. Curry is the father of two daughters and one son with his wife Ayesha, and he has discussed how his experience as a father and husband has shown him the importance of authenticity and equality. 'I encourage anybody who cares to listen, to embrace who you are, be yourself: that will be enough. You obviously have to work, you have to continue to evolve and grow, but we're all made unique and that will write your own story.'

Off the court, Curry is an advocate for women's rights, racial equality and social justice. On the court, he is an example of hard work, confidence and determination. A role model for sports fans and budding athletes, he reminds us why authenticity, perseverance and compassion are not only vital to both the professional and personal arenas, but needed now more than ever.

'If you take time to realize what your dream is and what you really want in life, no matter what it is, whether it's sports or in other fields, you have to realize that there is always work to do, and you want to be the hardest working person in whatever you do, and you put yourself in a position to be successful.'

Prologue

It's the summer of 2001, I'm thirteen years old and we're at the AAU (Amatuer Athletic Union) National Championships in Tennessee.

I was five-foot-five, five-foot-six tops – and maybe one hundred pounds soaking wet.

We lost badly, and I played worse.

I had finally gotten the chance that I'd been waiting for, all year, to measure myself up. And I fell short. Way short. It really felt like a wake-up call. It felt like this moment of truth – where there was only one possible lesson to take away: that I just wasn't good enough.

I remember getting back to our hotel room – I think it was a Holiday Inn Express – and just sulking. I wasn't being a hothead. I wasn't mad at losing. I was just . . . down. I was in my turtle shell. I guess I was feeling how we're really all taught to feel by these big tournaments, and this cutthroat basketball culture: like we're walking down some do-or-die path. My dad took that path, and he made it to the league. And his son? His son couldn't even make a mark against some other thirteen-year-olds.

So like I said, I wasn't heated. I was more just, 'Oh, okay. That's it? I'm not good enough? This is over?'

For me, in that moment, it pretty much *was* over.

But it was also in that moment that my parents sat me down – at that Holiday Inn in Tennessee – and gave me what I'd call probably the most important talk of my entire life.

I wish I had the transcript for you, since there were some real gems in there. Basically, though, my mom took the lead. She said, 'Steph, I'm only going to tell you this one time. After that, this basketball dream, it's going to be what it's going to be. But here's what I'll say: *No one* gets to write your story but you. Not some scouts. Not some tournament. Not these other kids, who might do this better or that better. And not *ever* your last name. None of those people, and none of those things, gets to be the author of your story. Just you. So think real hard about it. Take your time. And then you go and write what you want to write. But just know that this story – it's yours.'

Man, that moment stuck with me.

It stuck with me throughout my growing-up years, and it's stuck with me throughout my career as a basketball player so far. It's the best advice I've ever gotten. And anytime I've needed it – anytime I've been snubbed, or underrated or even flat-out disrespected – I've just remembered those words, and I've persevered.

I've said to myself, 'This is no one's story to write but mine. It's no one's story but mine.'

Wait – hold up. You didn't think this was one of those fairy tales where the kid gets some pep talk, and then immediately everything changes for the better, right? Because it *really* isn't that.

Man. I was still so far under the radar it was crazy.

I remember part of the problem being just how skinny I was. Like, I was so, so, so skinny. Could not put on that weight to save my life. Me and my cousin, Will, we used to walk down to the GNC [store] at this little shopping mall near our neighbourhood – just looking at the racks for some kind of miracle cure. We never had any money on us, so we wouldn't actually buy anything. But I guess we were just trying to . . you know what, I don't even know. Breathe in the magic GNC dust? We'd stay in there for twenty minutes, easy, staring at these giant tubs of mystery powder, like 'Must. Have. The Wheybolic.'

And then one day, out of the blue – it happened.

We got ripped.

Nah I'm kidding. We never, ever, ever got ripped. And honestly, other than growing a few inches, that was pretty much my scouting profile for the rest of high school: short, skinny, shoots some.

You can guess how it went over.

I remember the first look I got from a college, during my junior year – when Virginia Tech had some interest. Or I should say, when Virginia Tech showed some interest. If you squinted, it didn't seem *crazy* that they might want me: my dad went there, I'd made a few comments about how I'd like to go there and I was even finally starting to put up some numbers.

And when an assistant coach of theirs offered to swing by our school one day – to *meet* with me? Well, let's just say, I really squinted. I legitimately started to think they were going to make me an offer.

I suggested we meet 'over lunch' – cool move, right? Very professional. Except, I'm sixteen years old, at this small school with three hundred and sixty kids. And 'lunch' literally means 'in the cafeteria'. In front of the entire student body. So, maybe not so cool.

But the big day gets there, and it's finally lunch time. Their assistant coach walks in. He's got his big Hokies polo on. His big Hokies hat. We shake hands, and sit down, and – let's be really real – at this point I am straight-up feeling myself. *Whole school* seems like it's buzzing about me and my meeting. Got a room full of people doing the 'I'm not looking (I'm 100 per cent looking)' thing. It's basically a power lunch. I'm on top of the world.

And then, dude hits me with it. 'Yeah, so – Stephen, thanks for meeting. Really a pleasure. We'd like to invite you to walk on.'

Turns out, Virginia Tech was only meeting with me as – well, I wouldn't say a favour to my dad, like he would ever ask for that or anything – but it was more like, a courtesy?

'You have to have a passion about what you do. Basketball was mine and that's what's carried me to this point.'

A walk-on spot for the legend's son? I'd have to pay my own way. Or in other words: they were not interested.

*

I remember how humble our whole experience was at Davidson [College].

Which, first of all, is funny – because it's really nice now. Like, for real, if you're reading this, go to Davidson. It's an amazing school with an amazing hoops program. But back when I got there, what I mostly remember is just how loud and clear we all got the message that, you know – we were not playing Big-Time College Hoops. Man, like, we were *student* athletes. STUDENT in size one hundred font, athlete in size twelve font. We were 'Cool how you hoop and everything, but I'm going to need that philosophy paper' athletes. We shared a practice court with the volleyball team.

And then here was the gear rundown: two pairs of sneakers per year, two or three shirts – plus a pair of ankle braces. I honestly think that's it. One of my favourite memories to this day is of those Davidson practices when one of our new shoe shipments arrived. It was like a second Christmas. And then as far as the ankle-braces . . . man. That was a whole other situation. Let's just say, they were white at the beginning of the season. And by the end, they were not that colour.

It's love, though. Going to Davidson, and playing – and winning – at that level of hoops, it made me who I am, in a way. It made me understand what it means to build something. Like, truly build something. Something that no one can ever take away from you. Something that's all your own.

And it's interesting what I'll remember most about my time as a Wildcat. I'm sure everyone probably figures it's our win over Wisconsin in the Sweet Sixteen, or even our game versus Kansas in the Elite Eight.[v] But it's actually neither of those.

It's a memory from right in between them.

I was coming back from dinner, after practice – the night before we played Kansas. Just walking down the hall. And it was the strangest thing ever: I turned the corner down the hallway, and I ran into about half the team. The guys were sitting there, right on the floor, with their warm-ups on and their clunky 2007 laptops out. Like, this bunch of dudes that had just given back-to-back whoopings to Georgetown and Wisconsin. Sitting on the floor, typing away.

And I'm like, 'Umm, what are y'all doing?'

The whole group of them answer at the same time: 'Midterms.'

No, for real. That's a true story. It's twelve hours to the Elite Eight, twelve hours to the biggest game of any of our lives – and those boys were literally writing term papers in the hallway.

Straight up *grinding* in the Word doc. Man, I love Davidson with all my heart.

A while back, I had an idea.

It's called 'The Underrated Tour', and it basically goes like this: You've got all of these camps out there, right? All these basketball camps, across the country, around the world. And it's great, man. It's special. Those camps are how a lot of NBA guys originally made names for themselves. And we should keep that going! But there's another thing about these camps I've been thinking about. And it's how, if you take a closer look, you'll see that it's the same, exclusive group of kids participating in them, over and over. It's these same four- or five-star recruits, players every scout already knows, going from city to city, camp to camp.

And I guess I just got to thinking about how, you know, taking nothing away from those kids, those blue-chip prospects, but what about all the other kids? What about the kids who, for one reason or another, because of one perceived shortcoming or another, are getting labelled as two- or three-star recruits? Now I'm not saying those kids need to be at every camp. (Honestly, man, no one does.) But if we have it set up so those kids can't get invites to any camp? Then I think we've got a problem. Because then I think we're putting kids – kids who love to hoop, and who should be out there exploring that love – in a situation where a bunch of limits are being placed on them by other people. A situation where the limits of what they can accomplish are being put in place before they've gotten to test those limits for themselves.

And so that's the idea behind The Underrated Tour: to create a basketball camp for any unsigned high school players rated three stars and below. A camp for kids who love to hoop, and are looking for the chance to show scouts that their perceived weaknesses might actually be their secret strengths. And most of all? A camp for anyone who just isn't willing to let the rest of the world write their story.

I've noticed something.

It's how people assume that, once you've started to have a certain amount of success, 'feeling underrated' starts going away. And that, once you've finally reached any sort of ultimate goal, it starts going away forever.

But from my own experience? In your head, honestly – it never goes away.

In mine, it's never even diminished.

Not in 2010, trying to make five teams regret their draft decisions. Not in 2011, trying to show I'd have more value as a player than as a trade chip. Not in 2012, trying to fight through ankle problems. Not in 2013, trying to live up to a contract extension that a lot of people didn't think I deserved. Not in 2014, trying to prove these experts wrong who felt that *Curry's style of play just won't work in the playoffs*. Not in 2015, trying to prove these experts wrong who felt that *Curry's style of play just won't work in the ~~playoffs~~ finals*. Not in 2016, trying to break the Bulls' seventy-two win record.[vi] Not in 2017, trying to figure out how the Warriors blew a 3–1 series lead. Not in 2018, trying to overcome a mess of injuries and a good-as-hell Rockets[vii] team and whatever else got thrown our way. And not even in 2019 – man, not even this year – trying to hop out of the grave while people bury our historic run alive.

That chip on my shoulder has never gone anywhere. If anything, it's only become more and more a part of me.

And I think that's one of the biggest things I've really come to understand about myself over the last seventeen years: The way that *underrated* might start off as just some feeling the world imposes on you. But if you figure out how to harness it? It can become a feeling that you impose on the world.

And the more I think about it, the more I've realized that – above everything else – that

is why we've announced this. That's why
I've launched The Underrated Tour. Because
I already had one camp, and it's awesome, but
guess who wouldn't have been invited to it?

Me.

And I'll tell you what – I'm really starting
to see something in that dude.

Don't sleep on him.

Kid is a killer.

From "Underrated", The Players' Tribune, *10 January 2019*

'If I'm going to use my platform . . . I don't want to just be noise. I want to use it to talk about real issues, that are affecting real people. I want to use it to shine a spotlight on the things that I care about.'

The Interview

Could you please introduce yourself?

My name is Stephen Curry. I'm a father, husband, and a professional basketball player.

What really matters to you?

What really matters to me is my family in terms of the experiences that you have, the love that we get to share with each other, the support that we all have for each other. And that is where most of my happiness comes from in terms of being able to share life with people that you care about, that you love, and it gives you a sense of perspective about what you're doing in life.

Did you have a particular ambition or aspiration as a young person?

As I little kid I loved to do everything. I loved sports growing up. That was my first true love, and I loved to play a lot of different sports. I think that's where I learnt a lot about myself, developed my personality, my sense of confidence, and I think it propelled me

to, again, just find out how I could impact
people . . . especially with a unique talent that
I was given, in harnessing that from an early
age. But I was adventurous, I loved to have
new experiences and I just loved to have fun.
That was the main thing I guess that people
said about me the most – that I was always
smiling, always having fun.

Are you a dreamer? As a child, what was your
big dream?

Oh, I dreamt a lot. I think a lot of it was
centred around basketball at a young age
for sure. I just didn't know what that meant.
I knew that I loved to play, I knew that I loved
to work at it, and I knew that I had a natural
ability, but that down the road hopefully,
my dream would be to play in the NBA.
I didn't know what that meant in terms of
this life that I have now and the impact and
the platform that I have, but basketball is
definitely the seed that was planted early
and it's blossomed really nicely.

Has there been a special individual or individuals
that have particularly inspired you by their
example or wisdom?

For me at an early age it was always my
parents. I was blessed to have parents that
led by example but also taught me a level
of discipline and perseverance and work
ethic; that they didn't just do with words,
they actually showed by how they carried
themselves and the ambition that they had in
life. Then beyond that I've had so many great
coaches along the way that saw the best in
me and helped me get to my full potential,
and in the moment you don't really realize
how impactful they are because you're kind
of focused on what you're doing.

They're always there as sounding boards
but once you pass on to that next stage or
that next phase of life, you look back and
realize how truly impactful their example and
their commitment to my development was
through those very impactful ages. From
nine years old, when I first started playing
organized basketball, all the way through to
now in the NBA, I can think of five coaches

who have steered me in the right direction for different reasons, and I'm forever grateful for those people.

What were the values that your parents stood for that really made an impact on you, that you remember from your childhood?

Integrity was the biggest one. Being a good decision-maker and having a strong work ethic. [Those] were, I think, the three core values that they taught me, and understanding that I have a higher power that was looking down on me, or orchestrating every step that I took, and to have faith in that, no matter what I took on, what challenge I faced, or again, whatever ambition I had or dream I had. Even to this day I still chime in on that. But I understand that there're things out there that are way bigger than myself, and that again gives you a sense of gratitude and appreciation for everything that happens in your life.

Have you worked out a set of guiding principles
or a driving philosophy that underpins your life
and decisions?

Yeah, my faith is the driver of everything, and
when I think about something, a thought that
comes back every single day is 'I can do all
things through Christ who gives me strength'.
I write it on my basketball shoes before every
game; it's a practice that I do for myself in
terms of being able to have that confidence
that I can accomplish anything that I put my
mind to, but it's also turned into a sense of
inspiration I think for people who watch me
play. They look down at my sneakers and they
say, 'Oh, what's that Sharpie [marker pen]
line on there?' and they read it for themselves
and they can find a sense of confidence and
aspiration for themselves in whatever they
have going on in their lives. And so no matter
if it's on the court or off the court, in parenting,
in my marriage, I can do all things. No matter
if something happens, you know, what comes
at me or a challenge I have to face, I can get
through it.

'What really matters to me
is my family in terms of the
experiences that you have, the
love that we get to share with
each other, the support that we
all have for each other.'

Do you have daily disciplines and routines that are important to you?

For me it's more that I try to choose a perspective that I start the day with. That's the biggest thing for me – as crazy as life is, and I feel like I'm under a microscope every single day, no matter what kind of mood you're in or your energy level, I try to choose being positive and seeing the best in people, and again, having an appreciation for whatever the day brings. I think that sets me in the right direction. Some days it's harder than others, but I think that's important for me to be my best self and be the best version of myself and continue to grow. But having that choice every single morning, it's like, all right, how do you want to see the world today? Do you want to be positive, do you want to try to speak power over yourself in terms of what you're about to accomplish and what you're about to go through, as opposed to trying to be defeated and saying, 'Oh, woe is me.' I try never to have that attitude with anything.

Is there a process you have that helps you make that choice?

Yes. A lot of it has to do with my kids now and just looking in their eyes and they give me a smile or they'll say something, and that puts me in the right mood for sure, but a lot of it's just – it might not be right away when you wake up, it may be an hour into your day, it may take a little longer – but there's always that self-check moment where you're saying, 'Okay, you know, I haven't treated this day right, let's figure it out, let's get back to how I want to conquer the task at hand'. So you just have to be able to listen and be aware of how you're feeling in yourself, and I think for me it just depends on the day.

What qualities do you think have been most important for you in the achievement of your goals, both in your career and your life?

I mean, beyond just the sheer work that I've tried to put into my career and to the goals I put for myself, I think it is truly just a sense of gratitude and appreciation for everything that happens. I try to think that I'm the same person that I was as a kid and before any of this happened as I am now, in terms of just true appreciation for the experiences that I've had, the talents that I've been given, the people that I get to go to work with every single day, all the highs and lows. I think that's helped keep me moving in the right direction as opposed to getting complacent or, I call it, getting too big-headed, where I lose my sense of self and perspective. The biggest compliment that I've had in terms of that is that it seems like I have the same joy now that I did when I first started playing basketball. And no amount of fame or money or success will change that.

Is there a little part of you that says, 'I have to work harder than everybody else'?

Part of my basketball career and the journey has been that nothing was really given to me. I grew up in a basketball family and my dad played in the NBA, but the cards were pretty much stacked against me in terms of my physical stature and my abilities. I was never the guy that you could walk into a gym and see and say, 'Oh yeah, he's gonna be in the NBA'. I was the smallest kid on my team growing up and my work ethic was the thing that could help me close the gap on the talent and then separate me as I got into higher stages of basketball and higher levels. So, the part that I think I did the best at was whenever I got to that next level, the work multiplied and I knew that that was what was going to help me be successful. Even when I got into the NBA it was the same principle, and so eleven years into my NBA career I still have that mindset that, yes, I'm talented and I have natural ability, but the work that I put into it and the time and attention to detail, that carries all the weight for me.

What are the biggest lessons you have learned during the course of your life and career?

I think, to boil it down, it's that we're all special in some way, shape, or form, and to embrace that. I think for me it would have been easy to try to be something that I'm not, try to fit in or blend into the status quo, but I think there's been an extreme power in embracing

'What I tell people is be the best version of yourself in anything that you do. You don't have to live anybody else's story.'

my true self, my personality, what makes me special and unique, and letting that speak for itself. So, I'm truly proud of that in terms of all the variables that play out, you know, even different stereotypes within the NBA and how people see athletes in general, trying to break that – which is being myself. And I encourage anybody who cares to listen, to embrace who you are, be yourself: that will be enough. You obviously have to work, you have to continue to evolve and grow, but we're all made unique and that will write your own story.

How have you dealt with things that haven't worked out, when things have gone wrong, or plans haven't unfolded. How do you cope with that?

I've had plenty of those moments for sure. In sports that's bound to happen, but I've even been knocked down to the mat with injuries and surgeries and not knowing if I'd even be able to play basketball at the level that I wanted to play; I felt like it was kind of taken away from me. And those moments are when you truly identify your circle and

how important it is to find people that love
you for who you are, don't need anything
from you, don't want anything from you,
but will encourage you, uplift you, tell you
what you need to hear when you need to
hear it. Finding those people is extremely
important in life, you can't do anything alone.
I really have been blessed with a strong
circle that has got me through some really
tough times and some really dark, down
times, and I hope to be that [person] for other
people as well. But that – I guess you'd call it
community or family – it takes many different
shapes and sizes and forms, but we all need
those people that can root us and help us
when we're down.

What does leadership mean to you?

Leadership to me is just being selfless and
aware of how you impact people, and how
you can impact people. It takes different
styles of leadership: you can have the guys
or the gals that are really 'rah-rah' and can
use their words and be really vocal, you've
got leadership by example and everything in

between. I'm more of the lead-by-example type where I try to be the hardest worker in the room in terms of how that's going to separate me in the long term, understanding that no matter what's going on you have to be consistent with it. Our childhood upbringing was that somebody's always watching you – and that can be a story in itself – so I think I've gotten more comfortable in leadership in terms of whether it's some of my team, or my family, or what have you, but you're always learning, you're always growing. I think that's the common thread with great leaders, wherever they fall in the spectrum: they're always learning, they're always challenging themselves and they thrive mostly when it's uncomfortable too.

What do you think the world needs more of now?

Whoa! A lot. But I think overall, just positivity. I think if you look at certain world leaders and you look at social media and whatnot, negativity is just really loud. I truly believe that there's a lot of happiness and positivity going on, but it needs to be talked about more and shared more, and that will hopefully do wonders in terms of just keeping people upbeat and inspired. There's a lot of nastiness in this world, but there's also so many people doing amazing things and they're trying to change their communities on a local scale, an international scale, and everything in between. I'm actually preaching to myself right now! But continue to share more positive things that are happening in your life. And not being afraid to share those things, because they could impact one person or one million, and that's a win for sure. Yeah, hopefully the positivity is louder than the negativity.

What advice would you give your twenty-year-old-self?

I would tell him, one, buckle up because it's about to be a crazy ride, something that you probably would never – well, that you definitely didn't – expect. But it's going to be an amazing journey to impact people, and a very similar answer to the question earlier, just be yourself. At the end of the day that's going to win. Just be yourself. That's a good answer.

Epilogue

There's this miracle happening at home right now. And before it's over, I feel like I need to put it on paper – just to make sure I have some documented proof.

So let the record state: Riley, our six-year-old daughter, wants to be like her parents.

I know, I know – it's not going to last forever. And I know, that rebellious phase, it's coming. But for right now?

Well, we asked Riley, 'Hey, Ri Ri – what do you want to be when you grow up?' And she didn't miss a beat. 'A basketball player-cook.'

Like I said, the girl is really feeling her parents these days.

Now I won't lie: The last time we asked, it was between 'makeup artist' and 'horseback rider', so who really knows with this one. And I'm not going to pretend we have the logistics all figured out, either. Is she going to put out the cookbook first, and then start hooping? Or is she going to hoop first, and then turn to building her restaurant empire?

Either way, though, the skills are there. She's dribbling one hundred times in a row now – continuously – and we're working

on getting the left hand up to par. (Yes,
the jumper is legit.)

And then on the cooking front, Riley's
big thing is making everything: from pasta,
to cake, to eggs, to . . . slime. She has us set
up her camera while she's doing her thing in
the lab, and pretends like she hosts her own
YouTube show. It's crazy. I probably wouldn't
recommend eating the slime (too much glue),
but her fundamentals – they're already sound:
elite-level recipe-building, and a lot of really
creative colour choices.

Anyway, it's cool. And in all seriousness,
to have a daughter who thinks her parents are
alright-enough role models that she wants to
be like them – it's a blessing.

But at the same time, you know, Riley
arriving at that age – that age where she's really
starting to come into her own as a person – it's
also been a learning experience for me.

Growing up, I was lucky to be raised by my
mom, Sonya, an incredible and fiercely principled
woman who had the courage and vision to
open her own school, the Christian Montessori
School of Lake Norman.[viii] And for the last
seven years, I've been lucky to be married

to another incredible and fiercely principled
woman in Ayesha, who is both a successful
business owner and the most amazing mother
to our three kids. So for my whole life, really,
I feel like I've been receiving this education
on what it means to be a woman in America.

And one lesson from that education
that's really stood out to me is to always stay
listening to women, to always stay believing
in women, and – when it comes to anyone's
expectations for women – to always stay
challenging the idea of what's right.

In other words, I'd like to think that these
ideas have been on my mind for a while.

But even still.

Riley and Ryan are growing up so fast.
And with Ayesha and I suddenly seeing things
through the eyes of these daughters of ours,
who we brought into this world and now are
raising to live in this world, you know, I'd be
lying if I didn't admit that the idea of women's
equality has become a little more personal
for me, lately, and a little more real.

I want our girls to grow up knowing that
there are no boundaries that can be placed
on their futures, period. I want them to

grow up in a world where their gender does not feel like a rulebook for what they should think, or be or do. And I want them to grow up believing that they can dream big, and strive for careers where they'll be treated fairly. And of course, paid equally.

And I think it's important that we all come together to figure out how we can make that possible, as soon as possible. Not just as 'fathers of daughters', or for those sorts of reasons. And not just on Women's Equality Day. Every day – that's when we need to be working to close the pay gap in this country. Because every day is when the pay gap is affecting women.

And every day is when the pay gap is sending the wrong message to women about who they are, and how they're valued and what they can or cannot become.

Last week, I did something I'll never forget: I hosted a basketball camp for girls. Let's call it the 'first annual', actually, because I'm definitely planning on hosting one again. It was a lot of fun – just to share a court with two hundred girls who love to hoop, and watch them do their thing.

But I think it was also something more
than that. I think it was also the sort of thing
that can help to shift people's perspectives
so that when someone sees an NBA player
is hosting a camp now, maybe they won't
automatically assume it's for boys. And so
eventually we can get to a place where the
women's game, it isn't 'women's basketball'.
It's just basketball. Played by women, and
celebrated by everyone.

One thing we've always maintained about
our camp is that we want it to be world class.
And today? Here's the truth: you're not world
class if you're not actively about inclusion.

And like I said, the camp was incredible.
I've never seen a more engaged group of kids.
At every boys camp that I've ever been to,
you've always got some kids running around,
acting wild. But this camp, these girls, they
were about it. They were trying to absorb
every single thing. They were running up to me
after every drill, like, 'Steph, Steph, I got some
questions about how you trained as a kid. Can
you look at my form?' It was special, man.

And the girls didn't just bring it on the
court, they also brought it off the court. We

had a Q&A session with several successful women in sports and business, which historically have been fields dominated by men. And our campers blew me away with their questions. Just, like, the level of thoughtfulness and care that was flowing through them, and the maturity and nuance of it all. It really struck me.

One of the girls asked Ariel Johnson Lin, a VP at JPMorgan Chase & Co., about how, if she's in a business meeting, and has a great idea, but the meeting is composed of, say, eight men and then her as the only woman, would she think twice about how to convey the idea? Would she switch up how she worded things, or her body language, or her tone of voice, based on the gender imbalance of her workplace?

Again, I was just blown away. I mean, we're talking about a fourteen-year-old kid here, having the knowledge and sophistication to take a simple camp Q&A session to that level. And questions like hers, those really are the questions that young women continue to have to ask about the workplace today. And that's because it's still so deeply ingrained in them, even today, that inequality is just a thing you have to come to expect.

Ariel answered the question beautifully.

There was a long version, but I'll give you the short one, which was: 'Be yourself. Be good, and try to be great, but always be yourself.' You could see all of the girls at the camp nodding in unison, and I have to be honest – that was a really powerful moment for me. It was a satisfying feeling, to know we had put these girls in this position where they could connect with some role models, share their experiences and their ideas, and really just hoop, and be themselves. And feel like the main event.

But while that moment was satisfying, I'm not even close to satisfied. In fact, I'm feeling more driven than ever to help out women who are working toward progress, in any way that I can.

Let's work to close the opportunity gap. Let's work to close the pay gap.

And let's work together on this.

I mean, 'Women deserve equality' – that's not politics, right?

That's not something that people are actually disagreeing on, is it?

It can't be.

Earlier this summer, a few weeks after the season ended, Ayesha and I were blessed with the birth of our third child, Canon – our first son. And one of the things that has been most on my mind, since then, is the idea of what it means now to raise a boy in this world.

I already know, just based on his gender alone, that Canon will probably have advantages in life that his sisters can only dream of. How do you make honest sense of that as a parent? What are the values, in this moment, to instil in a son?

It's a lot to think about. But in the end, I think the answer is pretty simple.

I think you tell him the same thing that we told those girls last week at our camp: 'Be yourself. Be good, and try to be great, but always be yourself.'

I think you teach him to always stay listening to women, to always stay believing in women, and – when it comes to anyone's expectations for women – to always stay challenging the idea of what's right.

And I think you let him know that, for his generation, to be a true supporter of women's equality, it's not enough anymore to be learning about it.

You have to be doing it.

School's out. It's time to go to work.

From "This Is Personal", The Players' Tribune, 27 August 2018

About Stephen Curry

Stephen Curry is an American professional basketball player for the NBA's Golden State Warriors based in San Francisco, USA. He plays in the point guard position. His NBA career is marked by many firsts; he was the first person to be named Most Valuable Player by unanimous vote in NBA History and one of a select few to win MVP awards two years in a row. He holds six NBA all-star selections and three NBA Championships.[ix]

Curry was born in Akron, Ohio. His father Dell is a former NBA player who played for the Utah Jazz and Cleveland Cavaliers before Curry was born, later joining the Charlotte Hornets. Curry and his brother Seth watched their dad's games as children, and the family lived in Canada for a time while Dell played for the Toronto Raptors.

Curry played college basketball for the Davidson Wildcats after only being offered a walk-on position for his first choice, the Virginia Tech Hokies, due to his slight build. During his time with the Wildcats he set the team's all-time scoring record and was named SoCon Player of the Year twice. He also set the single-season NCAA record for the number of three-pointers made in his sophomore year.

In the 2009 NBA draft Curry was selected by the Golden State Warriors, who he continues to play for. He has been called the greatest shooter in NBA history by many sports critics and is often cited as revolutionizing basketball by encouraging teams to use the three-point shot to win. He is known for his incredible range, consistently taking shots from thirty to thirty-five feet.

In 2011 Curry married his long-term girlfriend, Canadian American Ayesha Alexander, a celebrity cook, restaurateur, television personality and cookbook author. They have three children.

With Ayesha, Curry launched the Eat. Learn. Play. Foundation in 2019 to help children succeed in life by combatting hunger, providing education and promoting active lifestyles.

Curry has won multiple awards, including the Jefferson Award for Outstanding Public Service in Professional Sports, the BET Award for Sportsman of the Year, and the ESPY Award for Best Male Athlete and Best NBA Player.

@stephencurry30
eatlearnplay.org

About the Project

'A true leader must work hard
to ease tensions, especially
when dealing with sensitive and
complicated issues. Extremists
normally thrive when there is
tension, and pure emotion tends
to supersede rational thinking.'

– Nelson Mandela

Inspired by Nelson Mandela, *I Know This to Be True* was
conceived to record and share what really matters for the
most inspiring leaders of our time.

I Know This to Be True is a Nelson Mandela Foundation
project anchored by original interviews with twelve
different and extraordinary leaders each year, for five
years – six men and six women – who are helping and
inspiring others through their ideas, values and work.

Royalties from sales of this book will support language
translation and free access to films, books and educational
programmes using material from the series, in all countries
with developing economies, or economies in transition,
as defined by United Nations annual classifications.

iknowthistobetrue.org

'A good head and a good heart are always a formidable combination.'

– Nelson Mandela

A special thanks to Stephen Curry, and all the generous and inspiring individuals we call leaders who have magnanimously given their time to be part of this project.

For the Nelson Mandela Foundation:
Sello Hatang, Verne Harris, Noreen Wahome, Razia Saleh and Sahm Venter

For Blackwell & Ruth:
Geoff Blackwell, Ruth Hobday, Cameron Gibb, Nikki Addison, Olivia van Velthooven, Elizabeth Blackwell, Kate Raven, Annie Cai and Tony Coombe

We hope that together we can help to mobilize Madiba's extraordinary legacy, to the benefit of communities around the world.

A note from the photographer

The photographic portraits in this book are the result of a team effort, led by Blackwell & Ruth's talented design director Cameron Gibb, who both mentored and saved this fledgling photographer. I have long harboured the desire, perhaps conceit, that I could personally create photographs for one of our projects, but through many trials, and more than a few errors, I learned that without Cameron's generous direction and sensitivity, I couldn't have come close to creating these portraits. I would also like to acknowledge the on-the-ground support of Matty Wong for helping me capture these images of Stephen Curry.

– Geoff Blackwell

About Nelson Mandela

Nelson Mandela was born in the Transkei, South Africa, on 18 July 1918. He joined the African National Congress in the early 1940s and was engaged in struggles against the ruling National Party's apartheid system for many years before being arrested in August 1962. Mandela was incarcerated for more than twenty-seven years, during which his reputation as a potent symbol of resistance for the anti-apartheid movement grew steadily. Released from prison in 1990, Mandela was jointly awarded the Nobel Peace Prize in 1993, and became South Africa's first democratically elected president in 1994. He died on 5 December 2013, at the age of ninety-five.

NELSON MANDELA
FOUNDATION
Living the legacy

About the Nelson Mandela Foundation

The Nelson Mandela Foundation is a non-profit organization founded by Nelson Mandela in 1999 as his post-presidential office. In 2007 he gave it a mandate to promote social justice through dialogue and memory work.

Its mission is to contribute to the making of a just society by mobilizing the legacy of Nelson Mandela, providing public access to information on his life and times and convening dialogue on critical social issues.

The Foundation strives to weave leadership development into all aspects of its work.

Notes

i   Wardell Stephen "Dell" Curry I (b. 25 June 1964), former professional basketball player. Played in the NBA from 1986 to 2002 for the Utah Jazz, Cleveland Cavaliers, Charlotte Hornets, Milwaukee Bucks, and Toronto Raptors.

ii   Stephen's grandpa, Jack Curry, passed away in 1990 when Stephen was two.

iii   Seth Adham Curry (b. 23 August 1990), professional basketball player for the Dallas Mavericks in the NBA.

iv   The athletic teams officially representing the Virginia Polytechnic Institute and State University (also known as Virginia Tech) in intercollegiate athletics.

v   The NCAA (National Collegiate Athletic Association) Division I Men's Basketball Tournament, also known and branded as NCAA March Madness, is a single-elimination tournament played each spring in the USA featuring sixty-eight college basketball teams. The first round, the First Four, eliminates four teams, and the remaining sixty-four teams play in thirty-two games over the course of a week, followed by the remaining Sweet Sixteen the following week, the Elite Eight the following weekend, then the Final Four.

vi   Chicago Bulls, NBA team based in Chicago, Illinois, USA. They won seventy-two games during the 1995–96 NBA season, setting an NBA record that was broken by the Golden State Warriors' seventy-three wins during the 2015–16 NBA season.

vii   Houston Rockets, NBA team based in Houston, Texas, USA.

viii The Christian Montessori School of Lake Norman in Huntersville, North Carolina, USA, was founded in 1995 by Dell and Sonya Curry.

ix   The NBA All-Star Game is an annual exhibition game played between the Eastern Conference and the Western Conference All-Stars, the two conferences that makes up the NBA. Twelve players are chosen from each conference – five starters and seven reserves. Starters are chosen by a combination of fans, media and current players, and reserves by the head coaches.

Sources and Permissions

1   Stephen Curry, "Underrated", theplayerstribune.com, 10 January 2019, https://www.theplayerstribune.com/en-us/articles/stephen-curry-underrated.

2   Rohan Nadkarni, "The NBA Has Never Seen a Shooter Like Stephen Curry", *Sports Illustrated*, 31 May 2018, https://www.si.com/nba/2018/05/31/stephen-curry-nba-finals-warriors-shooting-statistics.

3   Jack Holmes, "Steph Curry, Basketball Revolutionary, Is Starting to Chase Change Off the Court", *Esquire*, 5 April 2018, https://www.esquire.com/sports/a19672413/steph-curry-interview-trump/.

The publisher is grateful for literary permissions to reproduce items subject to copyright which have been used with permission. Every effort has been made to trace the copyright holders and the publisher apologizes for any unintentional omission. We would be pleased to hear from any not acknowledged here and undertake to make all reasonable efforts to include the appropriate acknowledgement in any subsequent edition.

Pages 6, 35: Stephen Curry, "The Noise", theplayerstribune.com, 12 November 2017, theplayerstribune.com/en-us/articles/stephen-curry-veterans-day; pages 12, 19–23, 26–29, 32–34: Stephen Curry, "Underrated", theplayerstribune.com, 10 January 2019, theplayerstribune.com/en-us/articles/stephen-curry-underrated; page 13: "The NBA Has Never Seen a Shooter Like Stephen Curry", Rohan Nadkarni, *Sports Illustrated*, 31 May 2018, si.com/nba/2018/05/31/stephen-curry-nba-finals-warriors-shooting-statistics; page 14: "Steph Curry, Basketball Revolutionary, Is Starting to Chase Change Off the Court", Jack Holmes, *Esquire*, 5 April 2018, esquire.com/sports/a19672413/steph-curry-interview-trump; pages 16, 24, 49: Golden State Warriors Media Conference, 4 May 2015, asapsports.com/show_conference.php?id=108794; pages 57–65: Stephen Curry, "This Is Personal", theplayerstribune.com, 27 August 2018, theplayerstribune.com/en-us/articles/stephen-curry-womens-equality; pages 73–74: *Nelson Mandela by Himself: The Authorised Book of Quotations* edited by Sello Hatang and Sahm Venter (Pan Macmillan: Johannesburg, South Africa, 2017), copyright © 2011 Nelson R. Mandela and the Nelson Mandela Foundation, used by permission of the Nelson Mandela Foundation, Johannesburg, South Africa.

First published in the United States of America in 2020 by Chronicle Books LLC.

Produced and originated by
Blackwell and Ruth Limited
Suite 405, Ironbank,150 Karangahape Road
Auckland 1010, New Zealand
www.blackwellandruth.com

Publisher: Geoff Blackwell
Editor in Chief & Project Editor: Ruth Hobday
Design Director: Cameron Gibb
Designer & Production Coordinator: Olivia van Velthooven
Publishing Manager: Nikki Addison
Digital Publishing Manager: Elizabeth Blackwell

Images copyright © 2020 Geoff Blackwell
Layout and design copyright © 2020 Blackwell and Ruth Limited
Introduction by Nikki Addison

Acknowledgements for permission to reprint previously published
and unpublished material can be found on page 83. All other text
copyright © 2020 Blackwell and Ruth Limited.

Nelson Mandela, the Nelson Mandela Foundation and the Nelson Mandela
Foundation logo are registered trademarks of the Nelson Mandela Foundation.

The views expressed in this book are not necessarily those of the publisher.

Library of Congress Cataloging-in-Publication Data available.

ISBN 978-1-7972-0019-4

Chronicle Books LLC
680 Second Street
San Francisco, CA 94107
www.chroniclebooks.com

10 9 8 7 6 5 4 3 2 1

Manufactured in China by 1010 Printing Ltd.